THIS BOOK BELONGS TO:

BOO!!

Dear Customer,

If you're using my product and finding value in it, I would greatly appreciate your feedback.

Please visit the product page on Amazon and select the 'Write a customer review' option.

Thank you for choosing my product - your satisfaction is my top priority.
I value my customer relationships and look forward to your valuable suggestions and feedback.

CONTENTS

"THE SECRET OF RAVENWOOD TRAIL"

In the small, sleepy town of Maplewood, nestled between rolling hills and dense forests, there was a trail that the locals rarely spoke about - Ravenwood Trail. Legend had it that the trail was home to strange and eerie happenings, especially on foggy nights.

The story of Ravenwood Trail was a popular one among the children at Maplewood's summer camp. They would gather around the campfire, their faces illuminated by the flickering flames, as the oldest counselor, Mr. Thompson, recounted tales of the trail's mysterious past.

Many years ago, he would begin, a group of explorers ventured into the trail but never returned. Some say they were swallowed by the mist, others believe they were spirited away by the creatures that lived deep within the woods.

One brave camper, 12-year-old Sarah, was fascinated by these stories. She decided to explore the trail herself, to uncover its secrets.

On a particularly misty evening, with a flashlight in hand and her heart pounding with excitement and fear, Sarah set off on the Ravenwood Trail.

The deeper she went, the more the forest seemed to change. The trees appeared to stretch endlessly into the sky, and the air was filled with an eerie silence, broken only by the occasional distant howl. Sarah felt as if the forest was watching her, its unseen eyes following her every step.

Suddenly, she stumbled upon an old, abandoned cabin hidden by overgrown vines. Curiosity overcoming her fear, Sarah stepped inside. The cabin was filled with old maps and strange artifacts, suggesting that it once belonged to the lost explorers.

As she examined the maps, Sarah realized they were marked with a path leading to a hidden part of the forest. Her adventurous spirit ignited, she followed the path marked on the map. The trail led her to a hidden clearing, where an ancient tree stood, its branches reaching out like twisted arms.

Beneath the tree, Sarah found a chest. Inside,

there were old journals belonging to the explorers, revealing that they had discovered a rare, magical plant that could heal any ailment. They had chosen to stay in the forest to protect this secret from those who would misuse it.

At that moment, Sarah felt a gentle breeze, and she heard a whisper in the wind, thanking her for uncovering the truth. She realized that the spirit of the explorers was still there, protecting the forest and its secrets.

Sarah returned to the camp, her mind swirling with the incredible discovery. She decided to keep the secret of the magical plant and the explorers, knowing that some mysteries were meant to be protected.

From then on, the story of Sarah's adventure on Ravenwood Trail became the most thrilling and talked-about tale around the campfire. The children of Maplewood would listen in awe and wonder, their imaginations running wild with the mysteries hidden within the depths of Ravenwood Trail.

"THE MOONLIT SHADOWS OF GRIMSWOOD FOREST"

In the quaint town of Willow Creek, nestled at the edge of Grimswood Forest, the children grew up hearing tales about the mysterious woods. Among these, the most spine-tingling was the story of the Moonlit Shadows.

Every full moon, the elders said, shadows danced under the silver glow in Grimswood. They whispered of a hidden realm within the forest, a place of secrets and spectral beings. The children, both scared and curious, would often dare each other to peek into the forest on full moon nights, but none dared to venture far.

Lucas, a brave and adventurous boy, decided to discover the truth behind these tales. One crisp autumn night, with a full moon high in the sky, he tiptoed out of his house with a small lantern in hand. His heart raced with a mix of fear and excitement as he approached the forest's edge.

As Lucas entered Grimswood, the world around him transformed. The trees seemed taller, their branches twisting into eerie shapes. The moon's cast long, dancing shadows that seemed to follow him. He heard faint whispers and soft giggles that seemed to come from nowhere and everywhere.

Venturing deeper, Lucas stumbled upon an ancient, gnarled tree, its bark etched with symbols that glowed faintly in the moonlight. The whispers grew louder, urging him to place his hand on the tree. As he did, the ground beneath him shimmered, and he was suddenly transported to a different part of the forest.

Here, in a clearing bathed in moonlight, stood a circle of stones, each engraved with the same strange symbols as the tree. In the center of the circle, a shadowy figure appeared. It was the Guardian of Grimswood, a spectral being who protected the secrets of the forest.

The Guardian spoke in a voice like rustling leaves, "Brave child, you have entered the heart of Grimswood. This place holds ancient magic, protected for centuries. You must promise to keep its secrets, for if they fall into the wrong hands, the balance of nature could be disrupted."

Lucas, awestruck and humbled, promised to

guard the secret. The Guardian smiled and gently touched Lucas's forehead. In that instant, Lucas was filled with visions of Grimswood's past and its mystical creatures.

He found himself back at the forest's edge, just as the first light of dawn crept into the sky. Rushing home, he knew he had a remarkable story to share at the next campfire gathering.

That night, as Lucas recounted his adventure, the children of Willow Creek listened in awe. His tale of the Moonlit Shadows of Grimswood Forest became a legendary story, passed down through generations. It was a tale of courage, mystery, and respect for the ancient magic that dwells in nature's hidden corners.

"THE ECHOES OF HOLLOW CREEK"

In the sleepy town of Elmwood, nestled among rolling hills, there lay a deep, winding creek known as Hollow Creek. Shrouded in mist and surrounded by gnarled trees, it was the centerpiece of the most bone-chilling campfire story known to the local kids.

The tale spoke of an old, forgotten mansion hidden deep within the woods around Hollow Creek. It was said that every Halloween night, strange echoes could be heard emanating from the mansion, as if the walls themselves were whispering ancient secrets.

One daring boy, 11-year-old Tyler, was both terrified and fascinated by this story. He decided to uncover the truth. On a chilly Halloween night, armed with nothing but a small flashlight and his curiosity, Tyler ventured towards Hollow Creek.

The moon cast eerie shadows on his path, and the sounds of the night seemed to grow louder with each step.

As he reached the creek, a dense fog settled around him, and the silhouette of the old mansion emerged through the mist.

Tyler's heart pounded as he stepped inside the mansion. The air was thick with the scent of old wood and mystery. As he explored the creaky halls, the whispers grew louder, guiding him to a grand, dusty library.

In the library, Tyler found an old diary belonging to the mansion's last inhabitant, a reclusive alchemist. The diary revealed that the alchemist had discovered a powerful elixir that could grant extraordinary knowledge but at a great cost. Fearing its power, the alchemist hid the elixir somewhere in the mansion.

Suddenly, Tyler heard a soft, ghostly voice. It was the spirit of the alchemist, bound to the mansion by his unfinished business. The spirit implored Tyler to find the elixir and remove it from the mansion, to prevent it from falling into the wrong hands.

Guided by the whispers, Tyler found a hidden chamber behind a bookshelf. There, on a pedestal, was the glowing elixir. Just as he reached for it, the mansion began to shake, as if trying to stop him. Tyler grabbed the elixir and ran, the mansion groaning and rumbling behind him.

He emerged from the mansion just as the first light of dawn broke through the night. The spirit of the alchemist appeared one last time, thanking Tyler for his bravery and freeing him from his earthly bonds.

Tyler returned to the campsite, the elixir safely in his possession. He buried it deep in the woods, where no one would ever find it. As he recounted his adventure by the campfire, the other kids listened in awe.

The story of Tyler's bravery and the Echoes of Hollow Creek became a legendary tale in Elmwood. It was a story of courage, mystery, and the thin veil between the ordinary and the extraordinary, perfect for those dark, starry nights around the campfire.

"THE SHADOW OF WHISPERING WOODS"

In a small town bordered by the dense, ancient Whispering Woods, children grew up hearing tales of the mysterious Shadow that lurked within. As autumn winds began to howl, these tales became the heart of every campfire gathering.

The most chilling story was about a young, adventurous girl named Lily, who was fascinated by the legends of the woods. Her curiosity peaked when she heard about the Shadow, a ghostly figure said to roam the forest, whispering secrets of the woods and guarding an ancient treasure.

One crisp October night, armed with a lantern and her dog, Max, Lily ventured into the Whispering Woods. The trees creaked and swayed as if conversing in hushed tones, and a mist curled around her feet. Lily felt a mix of excitement and fear, but her curiosity drove her deeper into the woods.

As the moon cast eerie shadows through the

branches, Lily stumbled upon a narrow, hidden path. Following it, she found herself in a clearing where the moonlight seemed to pool. In the center stood an old, twisted tree, its branches gnarled like outstretched hands.

Suddenly, a chill wind blew, and the Shadow appeared. It was a tall, wispy figure cloaked in darkness, with eyes that glowed like embers. Lily's heart raced with fear, but she stood her ground. The Shadow spoke in a voice like rustling leaves, "Why do you trespass in my woods?"

Lily, gathering her courage, replied, "I want to know the secrets of the woods, the truth behind the tales."

The Shadow considered her brave answer and then began to unveil the mysteries of the Whispering Woods. It spoke of ancient times, of spirits and creatures that dwelled within, and of a hidden treasure that held the essence of the forest.

But there was a warning: "The treasure must never leave the woods, for it is the heart of the forest. To take it would be to silence the whispers forever."

Guided by the Shadow, Lily discovered the treasure - a crystal that shone with an inner light. Overwhelmed by its beauty, she was tempted to take it but remembered the Shadow's warning.

Respecting the woods' secret, Lily left the crystal untouched. The Shadow, pleased with her choice, vanished into the mist, leaving Lily with a newfound understanding of the mysterious woods.

Lily returned to the campfire, her mind swirling with wonder. She shared her adventure, but kept the true secret of the Whispering Woods, knowing that some mysteries were meant to be protected.

The story of Lily and the Shadow of Whispering Woods became a legendary tale among the children. It was a story of bravery, curiosity, and respect for the unseen mysteries of the world, perfect for those dark nights around the campfire, where every shadow and whisper brought the legend to life.

"THE HAUNTING OF BLACK PINE TRAIL"

In the small town of Pine Ridge, nestled at the edge of an ancient forest, there was a narrow path known as Black Pine Trail. The trail was famous for its spooky campfire story, which every child in Pine Ridge knew by heart.

The tale began with an old legend about a hidden cave along Black Pine Trail, said to be the home of a mysterious creature known as the Shadow Beast. The creature was rumored to emerge on foggy nights, its eyes glowing like coals, and its howl echoing through the forest.

Despite their fear, a group of friends - Jack, Mia, and Sam - decided to explore Black Pine Trail one chilly October evening. Equipped with flashlights and a shared sense of adventure, they set off, their hearts pounding with both excitement and fear.

As they walked, the trees seemed to close in around them, casting long, eerie shadows in the moonlight. The forest was alive with strange noises - the rustling of leaves, the snapping of twigs, and a distant, unidentifiable howling that sent shivers down their spines.

Suddenly, a thick mist rolled in, enveloping the trail. The children could barely see a few feet ahead. That's when they heard it - a low, guttural growl coming from the mist. Panic set in as they realized they were not alone on the trail.

The growl grew louder, and out of the mist emerged the Shadow Beast, just as the legend described. It was a massive, wolf-like creature with fur as dark as the night and eyes that glowed eerily. The children froze in terror, but Jack mustered up the courage to step forward.

He remembered an old tale his grandmother had told him about the Shadow Beast. It was not a creature to fear but a guardian of the forest, protecting it from harm. Slowly, Jack extended his hand, showing that they meant no harm.

To their astonishment, the beast calmed down, its eyes softening. It let out a low, melodic howl, almost like a song, and then vanished into the mist as mysteriously as it had appeared.

The children hurried back to their campsite, their minds racing with what they had just experienced. They knew they had a fantastic story to share, one that would become a legendary tale around the campfires of Pine Ridge.

And so, the story of their encounter with the Shadow Beast of Black Pine Trail spread, a tale of bravery, respect for nature, and the mysterious creatures that dwell within it. It became a favorite among the children, a reminder that sometimes, the things we fear the most can be the most extraordinary.

"THE GHOST OF LANTERN HILL"

In the small town of Greenwood, nestled in the shadow of Lantern Hill, a chilling tale was passed down through generations. It was said that on certain foggy nights, the ghost of Old Man Winters, who once lived atop the hill, would wander, lantern in hand, searching for something he lost long ago.

The children of Greenwood would gather around campfires, their eyes wide with fear and fascination, as they listened to the story of Old Man Winters. He was a hermit, known for his love of rare artifacts and mysterious ways. One stormy night, he vanished, leaving behind only his flickering lantern on the hill.

Twelve-year-old Ellie, a brave and curious soul, was captivated by this legend. She decided to uncover the truth about the ghost of Lantern Hill. On a misty autumn evening, armed with a flashlight and a sense of adventure, Ellie ventured towards the hill.

As she climbed, the fog thickened, and the

silhouette of the old Winter's house emerged from the mist. The house was in ruins, but there was an eerie glow coming from the top floor. Ellie's heart raced as she stepped inside the creaky old house.

She followed the glow upstairs and found a room filled with old maps and artifacts. In the center of the room, there was a table with an ancient lantern casting a ghostly light. The air grew cold, and a shadowy figure appeared – the ghost of Old Man Winters, his face sorrowful and eyes searching.

Ellie, though scared, asked the ghost what he was looking for. The ghost's voice was a whisper, "My lost treasure, the rarest artifact I ever found. I cannot rest until it is returned to its rightful place."

Ellie promised to help. The ghost pointed to a map on the wall, where an X marked a spot in the forest. Ellie ventured into the woods, guided by the map. After hours of searching, she found a hidden cave. Inside, there was a chest containing a beautiful, glowing gem.

She returned to the house and gave the gem to the ghost. His face lit up with gratitude, and he vanished, finally at peace. The lantern's light flickered out, and the house was filled with a sense of calm.

Ellie returned to the campfire, her friends gathered around eagerly. She recounted her adventure, her voice filled with excitement and pride. The children of Greenwood would remember her tale for years to come, a story of bravery, mystery, and the power of kindness.

The legend of The Ghost of Lantern Hill evolved, no longer just a ghost story, but a tale of adventure and the unearthing of hidden truths, perfect for those dark, enchanting nights around the campfire.

"THE SECRET OF OLD CROW'S MANSION"

In the heart of the quiet town of Everwood, surrounded by thick, whispering forests, stood an ancient, abandoned mansion known as Old Crow's Mansion. The children of Everwood had grown up hearing hushed tales about the mansion, whispered around campfires under the cover of darkness.

Legend had it that Old Crow's Mansion was once home to a strange and reclusive man known as Mr. Crow. He was an eccentric collector of odd artifacts and rumored to dabble in mysterious sciences. One stormy night, many years ago, a bright light flashed from the mansion's highest tower, followed by a thunderous sound. After that night, Mr. Crow was never seen again, and the mansion stood silent, its secrets locked inside.

Tommy, a daring 12-year-old with a love for adventure, and his best friend, Lily, decided to uncover the truth about Old Crow's Mansion. As Halloween approached, they set out on a moonlit night, their hearts pounding with a mix

The mansion loomed before them, its silhouette casting a daunting shadow under the full moon. As they cautiously entered, the old wooden floors creaked under their feet. Cobwebs draped the walls like ghostly curtains, and the air was heavy with the scent of dust and forgotten times.

They explored the mansion, finding rooms filled with strange artifacts and old books. Suddenly, a cold breeze swept through the hallway, extinguishing their flashlights. In the darkness, they heard a faint, haunting melody playing from somewhere deep within the mansion.

Guided by the music, they found themselves in a grand library. An old piano in the corner played on its own, the keys moving as if pushed by invisible hands. Above the piano hung a portrait of Mr. Crow, his eyes seeming to follow them around the room.

Tommy noticed a peculiar book on a nearby shelf. As he pulled it out, a hidden staircase behind the shelf was revealed. With trepidation, they descended the stairs, which led to a secret underground laboratory filled with bizarre machines and glowing potions.

In the center of the lab stood a large contraption that looked like a portal. The machine suddenly whirred to life, and the ghostly figure of Mr. Crow appeared, trapped in an ethereal form. He explained that he had been experimenting with dimensional travel but became trapped between worlds.

Mr. Crow revealed that the only way to free him and close the portal was to find a special crystal hidden within the mansion. Tommy and Lily embarked on a frantic search, eventually discovering the crystal in a hidden compartment in Mr. Crow's bedroom.

As they placed the crystal into the portal machine, a blinding light filled the room. When their vision cleared, they saw that Mr. Crow's spirit had been set free, and the portal had closed. His last words, filled with gratitude, echoed in the now still mansion.

Tommy and Lily emerged from Old Crow's Mansion just as the sun began to rise. They hurried back to their campsite, eager to share their incredible adventure. Their tale of bravery and the mysterious happenings at Old Crow's Mansion became a legendary story in Everwood.

From that day on, the children of Everwood would gather around campfires, their eyes wide with wonder, as they listened to the thrilling tale of The Secret of Old Crow's Mansion, a story that blended fear with curiosity and adventure, perfect for those who dared to explore the unknown.

"THE MYSTERY OF ECHOING CAVE"

In the quaint town of Maple Hollow, nestled against the sprawling, dense forest of Whispering Pines, there lay a cave known as Echoing Cave. It was the heart of many campfire tales, each more spine-tingling than the last, especially the story of the Echoing Spirits.

According to legend, the cave was once home to spirits that communicated through echoes. Any word spoken inside the cave would be repeated in a chorus of ghostly whispers. It was said that if you listened closely, the spirits would reveal secrets of the past and future.

Curious and fearless, 12-year-old Emma and her best friend, Lucas, decided to explore Echoing Cave one autumn night. As they approached, the air grew cooler, and the sounds of the forest faded into an eerie silence.

With only their flashlights to guide them, they entered the cave. The walls were damp and covered in ancient cave paintings that seemed to tell a story. As they ventured deeper, their voices echoed, creating a symphony of whispers that sent shivers down their spines.

Suddenly, Emma stumbled upon a hidden alcove with a peculiar stone pedestal in the center. On the pedestal lay a strange, glowing orb. The moment she touched the orb, the cave lit up with spectral lights, and the echoes intensified.

The ghostly whispers became clearer, transforming into voices. These were the Echoing Spirits, trapped in the cave by a curse long ago. The spirits told Emma and Lucas that they were guardians of a powerful ancient artifact hidden within the cave, which had the power to control time.

The spirits warned them of a dark entity, known as the Shadow Wraith, that sought the artifact to plunge the world into eternal darkness. They pleaded with Emma and Lucas to find the artifact before the Shadow Wraith did, to break the curse and free the spirits.

Driven by courage and a sense of duty, the children embarked on a treacherous journey deeper into the cave.

They solved riddles and navigated through hidden passageways, each step taking them closer to the artifact.

Finally, in the heart of the cave, they found the artifact, a crystal emitting a soft, pulsing light. But at that moment, the Shadow Wraith appeared, a swirling mass of darkness with glowing red eyes.

In a daring act, Lucas distracted the Wraith while Emma placed the crystal back on its ancient altar. The cave trembled as light burst forth, banishing the Wraith and breaking the curse.

The spirits, now free, thanked Emma and Lucas, their voices fading into peaceful silence. The cave's eerie echoes were gone, replaced by a tranquil calm.

Returning to the campfire, the children shared their incredible adventure. The tale of The Mystery of Echoing Cave became a legendary story in Maple Hollow, passed down through generations.

This story of bravery, mystery, and the power of friendship would be told around countless campfires, inspiring awe and wonder in the hearts of children, a testament to the courage within each of us to face the unknown.

"THE PHANTOM OF FOGGY HOLLOW"

In the small, secluded town of Ravenwood, nestled at the edge of a dense, mist-laden forest known as Foggy Hollow, a chilling legend was whispered among the children. It was the tale of the Phantom of Foggy Hollow, a ghostly apparition that roamed the forest on moonless nights, its haunting cries echoing through the trees.

The story was a favorite at campfire gatherings, especially on breezy autumn nights when the mist from the forest crept into the town. It was said that the Phantom was once a woodsman who lived in the forest, guarding a mysterious, ancient relic hidden deep within the woods. One stormy night, he vanished without a trace, leaving behind only a trail of whispers and an unsolved mystery.

Twelve-year-old Max and his friends, Ava and Ethan, were both terrified and fascinated by this legend. Fueled by curiosity and a desire for adventure, they decided to unravel the mystery of the Phantom on a dark, moonless night.

Armed with flashlights, a map, and a sense of determination, the trio embarked on their quest. As they entered Foggy Hollow, the mist enveloped them like a cold, damp blanket. The forest was eerily quiet, save for the rustling of leaves and the distant hoot of an owl.

As they ventured deeper, they stumbled upon an old, abandoned cabin, its windows shattered and door hanging off its hinges. Inside, they found remnants of the woodsman's life – old tools, a dusty journal, and a faded photograph of a strange, glowing stone.

The journal revealed that the woodsman had been protecting the Heart of the Forest, a legendary stone said to hold the power of the forest itself. It was hidden in a secret chamber beneath an ancient tree marked with a carving of a raven.

Driven by the journal's clues, the children navigated through the twisting paths of Foggy Hollow. After what felt like hours, they found the ancient tree, its bark scarred with the distinct carving of a raven. Beneath the tree was a hidden trapdoor leading to a dimly lit chamber.

In the center of the chamber stood a pedestal, holding the Heart of the Forest – a radiant, emerald stone pulsating with a strange energy. As they approached the stone, a shadowy figure emerged from the darkness – the Phantom of Foggy Hollow.

The Phantom, with its hollow eyes and ghostly aura, spoke in a voice like the wind, "The Heart of the Forest must remain here, or the balance of nature will be disrupted." It revealed that the Phantom was the spirit of the woodsman, bound to the forest, protecting the stone.

Max, Ava, and Ethan promised to keep the secret of the Heart of the Forest. As they made their vow, the Phantom nodded solemnly and disappeared into the mist, its haunting presence finally at peace.

The children returned to the campfire, their hearts racing with the thrill of their adventure. They shared their story, but kept the secret of the Heart of the Forest, knowing that some mysteries were meant to be guarded.

The tale of The Phantom of Foggy Hollow became a legendary story in Ravenwood. It was a story that blended fear with wonder, teaching the children the importance of respect for nature and its hidden mysteries.

Around the campfires, as the mist from Foggy Hollow crept closer, the story was told and retold, a thrilling and haunting reminder of the adventure that lay in the shadows of the forest.

"THE ENIGMA OF SHADOW CREEK"

In the quaint, secluded town of Willowdale, bordered by the dense and whispering Evergreen Forest, there existed a creek as old as time itself, known as Shadow Creek. This creek, shrouded in perpetual twilight, was the centerpiece of a chilling campfire tale that had been passed down through generations.

The story was about the mysterious Shadow Beings, ghost-like entities said to guard an ancient secret hidden within the depths of Shadow Creek. It was believed that on nights when the moon was veiled by clouds, these beings emerged, whispering secrets of the past and future to those who dared to listen.

Jake, a bold and inquisitive 12-year-old, along with his friends, Mia and Alex, were captivated by this legend. Driven by a mix of fear and fascination, they decided to explore Shadow Creek on a foggy, moonless night, hoping to unveil its mysteries.

Equipped with lanterns and a map, they

cautiously navigated through Evergreen Forest, the silhouette of the trees casting eerie shadows in the dim light. As they neared the creek, the air grew colder, and an unnerving silence enveloped them.

The creek's water was still, reflecting the ghostly fog that hovered above. As they walked along its bank, they heard faint, ethereal whispers, sending chills down their spines. The whispers grew louder, guiding them to a hidden, overgrown path that led deeper into the forest.

Following the whispers, they arrived at a clearing where an ancient, gnarled tree stood. Beneath the tree was a small, stone well, its origins lost to time. The whispers beckoned them closer, urging them to look within the well.

Peering into the well, they saw not water, but a swirling vortex of light and shadow. Suddenly, the Shadow Beings appeared, their forms shifting and elusive. The beings spoke in a chorus of whispers, telling the tale of a powerful artifact, the Heart of the Forest, which was thrown into the well centuries ago to keep it from falling into the wrong hands.

The Shadow Beings warned that a malevolent force, known as the Dark Wraith, sought the Heart to control the forest and plunge the world into eternal darkness. They implored Jake, Mia, and Alex to retrieve the Heart and protect it.

Driven by courage, the children descended into the well, which led to an underground chamber illuminated by an ethereal glow. At its center was the Heart of the Forest, a crystal radiating with an inner light.

Just as they secured the Heart, the Dark Wraith appeared, a swirling mass of shadows with eyes like burning coals. In a daring confrontation, they outwitted the Wraith, using the light of the Heart to dispel the darkness and banish it.

Climbing out of the well, they found the Shadow Beings waiting. The beings, now at peace, thanked the children for their bravery. The Heart of the Forest was placed back into the well, its light sealing the chamber.

Returning to their campsite, the trio recounted their adventure. Their story of the Enigma of Shadow Creek became a legend in Willowdale, a tale that captured the essence of bravery, mystery, and the importance of preserving nature's balance.

Around the campfires, as the mist from Evergreen Forest crept closer, their story was told and retold, igniting the imaginations of children and adults alike, a thrilling and haunting reminder of the mysteries that lay hidden in the shadows of the world around them.

"A MYSTERIOUS EXPEDITION TO THE LOST FOREST"

In the small, quaint town of Pinevale, nestled at the foot of the Eldridge Mountains, there lay a dense, dark forest known as Eldridge Hollow. This forest was the heart of a bone-chilling campfire tale that had been whispered among the townsfolk for generations.

The legend spoke of the Cursed Woods, where shadows moved with minds of their own, and the trees whispered secrets of a time long past. It was said that an ancient spirit, known as the Guardian of the Hollow, protected a powerful amulet that held the balance between light and darkness.

12-year-old Sarah, along with her friends, Kyle and Emma, were always intrigued by this story. One crisp autumn evening, with the wind howling through the trees, they decided to explore Eldridge Hollow to uncover its mysteries.

Armed with flashlights and a hand-drawn map, they ventured into the woods.

The trees towered over them, their branches clawing at the sky, and the air was filled with the scent of decay and mystery. An eerie fog crept along the ground, enveloping their feet as they walked deeper into the forest.

As they delved further, the forest grew darker, and a chilling silence enveloped them. Suddenly, they heard a soft, haunting melody echoing through the trees. Curiosity overcoming their fear, they followed the sound to a clearing where an old, decrepit cabin stood.

The melody seemed to emanate from the cabin. Cautiously, they stepped inside, finding the interior surprisingly intact. In the center of the room, a dusty, ancient book lay open on a table, its pages fluttering in the breeze.

The book told the tale of the Guardian of the Hollow, a powerful spirit who had once been a wise sage. He had created the amulet to keep the forces of darkness at bay but had fallen victim to its curse, becoming bound to the forest forever.

As they read, the air grew colder, and a shadowy figure appeared before them - the Guardian of the Hollow. His eyes glowed with a spectral light, and his voice was like the rustling of leaves. "The amulet must never leave these woods," he warned, "for its power is too great for the outside world."

He told them of a dark entity, known as the Shadow Walker, that sought the amulet to unleash chaos. The children, realizing the gravity of the situation, vowed to protect the amulet.

Guided by the Guardian, they journeyed deeper into the woods, where the trees seemed to twist and contort, forming a labyrinth. At its heart lay an ancient altar, upon which the amulet rested, pulsing with a strange energy.

As they approached, the Shadow Walker emerged from the darkness, a creature of nightmares with eyes like burning embers. In a moment of fear and courage, they used the light from their flashlights to create a barrier of light, holding the creature at bay.

Working together, they secured the amulet, and the Guardian appeared once more. He thanked them, his spirit finally at peace, as he faded into the forest. The children returned the amulet to its altar, where it would remain safe, its power contained.

Exhausted but triumphant, they made their way back to their campsite. The story of their adventure in the Cursed Woods of Eldridge Hollow became a legendary tale in Pinevale, a story of bravery, mystery, and the eternal battle between light and darkness.

Around the campfires, as the wind whispered through the trees, their tale was told and retold, a thrilling and chilling reminder of the mysteries that lay hidden in the shadows of the forests and in the hearts of the brave.

"THE WHISPERER IN THE WOODS"

In the remote town of Aspen Grove, surrounded by dense, towering forests, there was a legend that sent shivers down the spines of all who heard it. It was the story of the Whisperer in the Woods, a spectral figure that roamed the forest, its eerie whispers carried by the wind on moonless nights.

The tale was a campfire staple, particularly among the children at Camp Pineledge. They would gather around the crackling fire, eyes wide with a mix of fear and fascination, as the oldest counselor, Mr. Thompson, recounted the story.

The Whisperer was once a lumberjack named Old Man Harris, who lived in a small cabin deep in the woods. One stormy night, after venturing into the forest, he mysteriously vanished. Some said he was taken by the forest itself, others believed he stumbled upon a forbidden ancient secret.

Twelve-year-old Lily, an intrepid and curious

girl, along with her friends, Ben and Hannah, decided to uncover the truth about the Whisperer. Armed with flashlights, a compass, and their courage, they set out into the forest on a moonless night.

As they ventured deeper, the forest seemed to come alive. Shadows danced between the trees, and strange sounds echoed around them. The air grew colder, and a thin mist swirled at their feet.

Suddenly, they heard it - a faint whisper, almost like a sigh, moving through the trees. They followed the sound, which seemed to beckon them deeper into the forest. The whispers grew louder, leading them to an old, overgrown path rarely trodden by the townsfolk.

The path led to a clearing, where stood the ruins of Old Man Harris's cabin. As they approached, the whispers ceased, and a profound silence fell over the woods. The cabin, though decrepit, still held remnants of its past - a rusty axe, a worn-out hat, and a tattered journal.

Hannah, braver than the rest, picked up the

journal. It contained the ramblings of Old Man Harris, speaking of a hidden cavern beneath the forest, where a mystical spring flowed. This spring was said to grant visions of the future but at a terrible cost.

Driven by curiosity, the children discovered a hidden trapdoor beneath the cabin's floorboards, leading to a narrow, winding tunnel. They followed the tunnel until it opened into a vast, underground cavern, illuminated by glowing crystals.

In the center of the cavern was the spring, its waters shimmering under the crystal light. Lily, Ben, and Hannah, mesmerized by the sight, heard the whispers again, now clear and beckoning them to drink from the spring.

Remembering Old Man Harris's warning, they resisted the temptation. Suddenly, the Whisperer appeared, a ghostly figure shrouded in mist, its eyes filled with sorrow. It spoke in a voice that echoed the wind, revealing itself as the spirit of Old Man Harris.

He had drunk from the spring, seeking knowledge, but was cursed to remain in the forest, bound to the spring's power. He warned the children to leave and never return, to avoid his fate.

They heeded his warning, leaving the cavern and making their way back to the camp. As they reached the safety of their campfire, the forest behind them seemed to sigh, the Whisperer's presence fading into the night.

Back at the camp, the tale of their encounter with the Whisperer in the Woods became a new legend, a tale of bravery, mystery, and the importance of respecting the unknown. Around the campfires, as the wind whispered through the trees, their story was told and retold, a thrilling and chilling reminder of the adventures and mysteries that lay hidden in the darkness of the woods.

"THE SHADOWS OF MOONLIT GLEN"

In the sleepy town of Willow Creek, nestled among the dense, misty woods of Moonlit Glen, there whispered a tale that sent shivers down the spines of those who dared to listen. The tale was about the mysterious, haunting Shadows of Moonlit Glen, ghostly figures that appeared only on nights when the moon shone full and bright.

The children of Willow Creek, especially those at Camp Nightwood, would gather around the campfire, their eyes wide with anticipation as the camp leader, Mr. Jacobs, recounted the legend in hushed tones.

Many years ago, Moonlit Glen was home to a lively village. But one fateful night, under a full moon, a strange mist descended upon the village, and with it came the Shadows. These ghostly figures roamed the streets, their eerie whispers echoing in the night air. By morning, the village was deserted, its inhabitants vanished without a trace.

Intrigued and undeterred by the ominous tale, three brave friends - Ellie, Jack, and Mia

- decided to uncover the truth behind the Shadows of Moonlit Glen. One full moon night, armed with flashlights and a camera, they ventured into the heart of the glen.

As they delved deeper, the moon cast a silvery glow over the woods, creating a surreal, otherworldly atmosphere. A thick mist began to rise from the ground, swirling around their feet. It was then they first heard it - a soft, haunting melody, drifting through the trees.

Following the melody, they stumbled upon the ruins of the old village. The buildings were overgrown with vines, and an eerie stillness hung in the air. In the center of the village square stood an ancient stone well, its edges worn by time.

As they approached the well, the Shadows appeared, their forms wispy and translucent, moving with the grace of the wind. The children stood frozen in awe and fear as the Shadows began to circle the well, their whispers growing louder.

The Shadows were not malevolent spirits, as the legend suggested, but guardians of a secret. They revealed through whispered song that the well was a gateway to another realm, a world parallel to our own, where time stood still.

The villagers, they explained, had discovered this gateway and chose to enter the new realm, seeking a life free from the troubles of the outside world. The Shadows were left behind to guard the well and ensure that the secret remained hidden.

However, they warned that the gateway was unstable and that crossing over could mean being lost in between worlds forever. The children, heeding the warning, promised to keep the secret of Moonlit Glen.

With a newfound respect for the legend and its guardians, Ellie, Jack, and Mia made their way back to the camp. Around the fire, they shared their adventure, transforming the tale of the Shadows of Moonlit Glen from a ghost story to a mystical legend of guardianship and hidden worlds.

The story became a campfire favorite, a tale of bravery, curiosity, and the unseen wonders that lurk in the shadows of the moonlit night. It reminded the children of Willow Creek that sometimes, the most extraordinary adventures and mysteries are hidden in plain sight, waiting to be discovered by those brave enough to look.

"THE FORGOTTEN ECHOES OF HOLLOW VALE"

In the quaint, tucked-away town of Evergreen Hollow, surrounded by thick, shadowy woods, there was a legend known to chill the bones of all who heard it. It was the story of the Forgotten Echoes of Hollow Vale, a spectral phenomenon that occurred in the deepest part of the woods known as Hollow Vale.

Camp Evergreen, situated at the edge of these woods, was a place where children gathered around campfires, their eyes wide with a mix of fear and curiosity, as the camp counselor, Mr. Dawson, told tales of the forgotten echoes.

The legend had it that many years ago, Hollow Vale was a bustling settlement, but a mysterious curse befell it. One by one, the villagers began to disappear, leaving behind only their echoing voices, trapped in the fabric of the forest. It was said that on certain nights, when the moon was just a sliver in the sky, one could hear their whispers and cries, a haunting reminder of the village that once was.

Driven by a blend of fear and fascination, three friends—Sophie, Liam, and Aiden—decided to explore Hollow Vale. As they ventured into the woods one chilly autumn evening, the trees seemed to close in around them, and a dense fog crept along the ground.

Their journey led them deeper into the woods than they had ever been. The air grew colder, and a sense of unease settled over them. That's when they first heard it: faint whispers, like echoes of a distant conversation, drifting through the trees.

Following the whispers, they came across the ruins of the old village. Overgrown and long forgotten, the village was a maze of crumbling buildings and deserted streets. In the center of the village stood an ancient, gnarled tree, its branches reaching out as if trying to speak.

As the children approached the tree, the whispers grew louder and more distinct. They realized that these were the voices of the villagers, forever bound to the woods, endlessly recounting the days of their lives and their tragic fates.

Suddenly, the ground beneath them began to

tremble, and a ghostly figure emerged from the tree—a spectral apparition of the village's last elder. In a voice that was both a whisper and a wail, the elder recounted the tale of the curse that had befallen Hollow Vale. A powerful entity, known as the Shadow Wraith, had sought to claim the woods for itself, casting the village into an eternal twilight.

The elder revealed that the only way to break the curse and free the voices was to find a hidden amulet, the Heart of the Vale, and return it to its rightful place in the heart of the forest.

Guided by the whispers, Sophie, Liam, and Aiden embarked on a quest through the spectral village. They navigated through the eerie, abandoned houses and down shadowy lanes until they found the amulet, glowing with an otherworldly light, hidden beneath an old floorboard in the elder's house.

As they retrieved the amulet, the Shadow Wraith appeared, a swirling mass of darkness and malice. In a heart-pounding moment of bravery, the children held up the amulet, its light piercing the darkness. The Wraith let out a piercing scream and vanished, the curse lifting from the woods.

The children returned the amulet to its place beneath the ancient tree. As they did, the whispers faded away, leaving a peaceful silence in their wake. The spirits of Hollow Vale were finally at rest.

Upon returning to Camp Evergreen, the trio recounted their harrowing adventure. Their tale of the Forgotten Echoes of Hollow Vale became a legendary story at the camp, a haunting and thrilling tale of bravery, mystery, and the enduring power of friendship.

Around the campfires, as the night wind whispered through the trees, their story was told and retold, a chilling and mesmerizing reminder of the adventures that lie hidden in the shadows, waiting for the brave to uncover them.

"THE HAUNTING OF RAVEN'S HOLLOW"

In the small, secluded town of Pine Bluff, surrounded by dense, dark forests, there was a place shrouded in mystery and fear - Raven's Hollow. The children of Pine Bluff grew up listening to the spine-chilling tale of the haunting in these woods, a story that became the highlight of every campfire.

The legend spoke of an old, abandoned house in the heart of Raven's Hollow, hidden away from the world. It was said that every year, on the night of the Harvest Moon, the house came to life with the echoes of its dark past, haunted by the ghost of its former owner, Old Man Craven.

Intrigued and daring, 13-year-old Max, his sister Lily, and their friend Jake decided to uncover the truth about the haunted house. On the night of the Harvest Moon, armed with flashlights and a camera, they ventured into Raven's Hollow.

As they made their way through the thick woods, an eerie silence enveloped them.

The trees seemed to whisper secrets of the past, and a cold wind nipped at their heels. Finally, they reached the old house, its windows dark, its structure crooked and unwelcoming.

As they stepped inside, the door creaked shut behind them, plunging them into darkness. Their flashlights flickered as they explored the dusty, cobwebbed rooms. The air was thick with the scent of decay and long-forgotten memories.

Suddenly, they heard a faint sound - a piano playing from the upper floor. Heart racing, they followed the music to a dimly lit room where an old piano sat. As Max approached, the music stopped abruptly, and the room grew colder.

Lily noticed a portrait on the wall of Old Man Craven. His eyes seemed to follow them, filled with sorrow and regret. Beneath the portrait, they found a diary. It told the tragic tale of Old Man Craven, who was once a kind and prosperous man, but lost everything he loved to a mysterious illness that swept through the Hollow.

As they read, a ghostly figure appeared - the apparition of Old Man Craven. He spoke in a hushed, tormented voice, telling them that he was bound to this world by his unresolved sorrow and the secrets buried within the house. He revealed that the only way to free his spirit was to find a hidden locket, the last memento of his lost family, and return it to its rightful place in the family crypt behind the house.

Driven by a desire to help, the children searched the house and found the locket hidden in a secret compartment in the wall. As they placed the locket in the crypt, a warm, glowing light enveloped the area, and the ghost of Old Man Craven smiled peacefully, finally released from his earthly bonds.

The children emerged from the house just as dawn broke, the house now silent and still. They returned to their campsite, their hearts filled with a mix of fear and triumph.

Their tale of the Haunting of Raven's Hollow became a legendary story in Pine Bluff, a tale of adventure, mystery, and the power of empathy and courage. Around the campfires, as the wind rustled through the trees, their story was told and retold, a thrilling and chilling reminder of the mysteries that lay hidden in the shadows and the legacy of the past that shaped them.

"THE LEGEND OF SHADOW GLEN"

In the quaint town of Cedar Falls, nestled between rolling hills and dense woodlands, there was a place steeped in mystery and fear - Shadow Glen. Known for its chilling campfire story, Shadow Glen was the subject of many hushed conversations among the children of Cedar Falls.

The story was about the mysterious 'Night Walker' of Shadow Glen, a ghostly figure rumored to roam the woods on moonless nights. It was said that this spectral entity was once a villager who had ventured too deep into the Glen and stumbled upon an ancient, forbidden secret.

Eager to uncover the truth, three brave friends, Zoe, Ethan, and Mia, decided to explore Shadow Glen one foggy autumn night. Armed with lanterns, a map, and a shared sense of adventure, they set out into the heart of the woods.

As they delved deeper, the trees seemed to

close in around them, casting eerie shadows in the faint light. An unsettling silence pervaded the air, broken only by the occasional rustle of leaves. The fog grew thicker, making it almost impossible to see more than a few feet ahead.

Suddenly, they heard a soft, haunting melody drifting through the trees. Compelled by curiosity, they followed the sound to a clearing where an old, abandoned cottage stood. Its windows were dark, and the door creaked ominously in the wind.

Inside, they found remnants of a life long forgotten - a dusty piano, faded photographs, and a diary lying open on a table. The diary belonged to Jonathan Harker, the villager who had become the Night Walker. His writings spoke of a hidden underground chamber in Shadow Glen, where an ancient artifact was kept.

This artifact, the Heart of the Glen, was said to hold the power to control the forest and was guarded by the spirits of the woods. Jonathan had tried to take the artifact, believing it would bring prosperity to the village. Instead, it cursed him to roam the woods as the Night Walker, forever bound to the Glen.

Determined to help Jonathan find peace, the children searched for the hidden chamber. Guided by clues in the diary, they discovered a trapdoor beneath the cottage's floor, leading to a narrow, winding staircase that descended into darkness.

At the bottom of the staircase lay the chamber, illuminated by a faint, otherworldly glow. In its center stood a pedestal, upon which the Heart of the Glen, a shimmering, emerald-like stone, rested.

As they approached, the ghostly figure of Jonathan Harker appeared, his eyes filled with sorrow and warning. He explained that removing the Heart of the Glen would unleash the wrath of the forest spirits. The only way to break the curse was to vow to protect the forest and its secrets.

Zoe, Ethan, and Mia promised to guard the secret of Shadow Glen and its ancient power. As they made their vow, Jonathan's spirit was enveloped in a gentle light, and he vanished, his curse finally lifted.

The children emerged from Shadow Glen just as dawn broke, their hearts heavy with the night's revelations. They returned to their campsite and shared their adventure, turning the tale of the Night Walker into a story of bravery, mystery, and the importance of respecting nature.

Their story of the Legend of Shadow Glen became a campfire classic in Cedar Falls, a thrilling and haunting reminder of the adventures that await in the shadows of the night and the mysteries that linger in the whispering woods.

"THE SECRET OF BLACKWOOD TRAIL"

In the small, serene town of Oakhaven, bordered by the ancient and sprawling Blackwood Forest, there was a tale that intrigued and terrified every child who heard it. It was the story of Blackwood Trail and the mysterious entity known only as "The Whisperer."

For generations, the tale of The Whisperer had been a staple of campfire stories at Camp Oakhaven. The legend spoke of a shadowy figure that roamed the Blackwood Trail, a path winding deep into the heart of the forest. It was said that those who walked the trail after dusk could hear The Whisperer's faint, eerie murmurs, carrying secrets and omens.

Eager to uncover the truth, three courageous friends, Sarah, Luke, and Emma, decided to explore Blackwood Trail one cool October evening. Equipped with flashlights, a map, and a boundless curiosity, they ventured into the forest as the sun began to set.

As they walked, the forest seemed to grow denser, the trees towering high above, their branches interlocking like fingers. A thick mist settled over the trail, and the world around them grew eerily quiet, save for the crunch of leaves underfoot.

As night fell, they reached the heart of Blackwood Trail. That's when they first heard it: a soft, whispering voice, like the rustling of leaves. It seemed to come from all around them, echoing through the trees. The children felt a chill run down their spines but were determined to continue.

Following the sound, they came upon an ancient, gnarled tree, larger than any they had ever seen. The whispers grew louder, and they realized the tree was the source. Beneath the tree, partially buried in the earth, was an old, weathered chest.

With bated breath, they opened the chest and found inside a collection of old, handwritten journals. The journals belonged to the original settler of Oakhaven, a woman named Abigail Blackwood. As they flipped through the pages, they uncovered the truth about The Whisperer.

Abigail had discovered a rare, mystical plant in the forest, which had the power to grant visions of the future. She had used it to protect the town, but over time, the plant's power had grown too strong, binding her spirit to the forest as its guardian. She became The Whisperer, destined to roam the trail, guiding and warning those who dared to walk it.

Determined to help Abigail find peace, the children searched for the mystical plant, guided by clues in her journals. Deep within the forest, they found the plant, its leaves shimmering under the moonlight.

The children heard Abigail's voice once more, thanking them and asking them to remove the plant from the forest, thus breaking her bond. With a mixture of awe and fear, they carefully uprooted the plant and carried it away from Blackwood Trail.

As they did, a gentle light enveloped the area, and the spirit of Abigail Blackwood appeared before them. She smiled serenely and vanished, her whispers fading into the night air.

The children emerged from the forest just as dawn broke, their hearts filled with a mix of fear and pride. They returned to Camp Oakhaven and shared their incredible adventure, turning the tale of The Whisperer into a story of bravery, mystery, and the power of compassion.

Their story of The Secret of Blackwood Trail became a legendary tale at Camp Oakhaven, a thrilling and chilling reminder of the mysteries that lay hidden in the forests and the courage it takes to uncover them. Around the campfires, as the wind whispered through the trees, their story was told and retold, a captivating and haunting tale for all who dared to listen.

"THE CURSE OF MILENT WILL"

In the cozy town of Maple Ridge, overshadowed by a towering, fog-covered hill known as Milent Will, a harrowing legend was passed down through generations. This legend, a staple of campfire stories, told of the haunting Curse of Milent Will.

The story began long ago, with an old mansion perched atop the hill, hidden by the dense fog. It was said that the mansion was cursed, and on moonless nights, eerie lights and strange shadows could be seen through the mist, while ghostly whispers echoed in the wind.

Three friends, adventurous 12-year-old Jake, his courageous sister Lily, and their clever friend Max, were intrigued by the legend. Fueled by a blend of fear and curiosity, they decided to venture to Milent Will one chilly autumn evening to uncover the truth.

Armed with flashlights, a map, and a walkie-talkie, they began their ascent up the winding path leading to the hill. As they climbed, the fog grew thicker, and a haunting silence enveloped them. The only sound was their footsteps crunching on the fallen leaves.

Upon reaching the summit, they found the old mansion, its gates creaked open, inviting them into its dark, mysterious halls. The mansion was a labyrinth of dusty rooms and creaky floors, filled with old portraits and antique furniture.

As they explored, they stumbled upon a hidden room with a large, ancient book on a pedestal. The book, bound in faded leather, told the tale of the mansion's original owner, a reclusive alchemist named Lord Ravenswood, who was rumored to have dabbled in dark magic.

Lord Ravenswood had created a powerful amulet, the Heart of the Will, which he believed could control the forces of nature. However, his experiment went awry, unleashing a curse upon the mansion and trapping his spirit within its walls.

The children realized that the strange occurrences on Milent Will were manifestations of the curse and that the only way to break it was to find the amulet and release its energy.

Guided by clues in the book, they searched the mansion, their journey taking them through secret passages and dusty libraries. Finally, in a hidden chamber beneath the mansion, they found the amulet, glowing with an eerie light.

As they approached, the ghost of Lord Ravenswood appeared, a spectral figure filled with sorrow and regret. He warned them that releasing the amulet's power would also awaken the spirits bound to the mansion, who would try to stop them.

With bravery and quick thinking, the children worked together to release the amulet's energy. The mansion shook as the spirits emerged, wailing and swirling around them. Jake, Lily, and Max held the amulet high, and a blinding light filled the room.

When the light faded, the spirits were gone, and the mansion was silent. They had broken the curse, freeing Lord Ravenswood and the other spirits from their eternal bondage.

Exhausted but triumphant, the children returned to their campsite as the first light of dawn broke over the hill. They shared their incredible adventure, turning the tale of

The Curse of Milent Will into a legendary story of courage, friendship, and the triumph over darkness.

Around the campfires of Maple Ridge, their story was told and retold, a thrilling and chilling reminder of the adventures that lie hidden in the shadows and the power of unity in the face of fear.

"THE EYES OF THE FOREST"

In the quaint town of Pinebrook, nestled at the edge of the ancient and whispering Everpine Forest, there circulated a chilling tale that had captivated the imaginations of children for generations. This tale, often shared around crackling campfires under the starry sky, was known as "The Eyes of the Forest."

The story began with an old legend about the forest's guardian - a mysterious entity known as the Green-Eyed Watcher. It was said that on nights when the moon was hidden behind thick, dark clouds, the Watcher would emerge, its glowing green eyes visible through the dense foliage of Everpine Forest.

Curiosity and a hint of fear spurred a brave group of friends - twelve-year-old Alex, his spirited sister Jenna, and their resourceful friend Tyler - to uncover the truth behind this enigmatic guardian. One cloudy, moonless night, armed with flashlights and a sense of adventure, they ventured into the heart of Everpine Forest.

As they made their way through the forest, the thick trees seemed to close in around them, creating a maze of shadows and whispers. An eerie fog crept along the forest floor, and the only sound was the crunch of leaves under their feet.

Deeper into the forest, they stumbled upon a clearing where the fog seemed to swirl around a particular spot. There, they saw it - a pair of luminescent green eyes, floating in the darkness. Fear gripped them, but they stood their ground, fascinated by the sight.

As they watched, the eyes slowly morphed into the form of a grand, ethereal stag, its antlers stretching wide and adorned with shimmering leaves. The Green-Eyed Watcher had revealed itself, not as a menacing spirit, but as a majestic protector of the forest.

The Watcher spoke in a voice that rustled like leaves, telling them of a time when the forest was threatened by a darkness that sought to consume its life. It had been a guardian for centuries, watching over Everpine, ensuring that the balance of nature was maintained.

However, the Watcher's strength was waning,

for the heart of the forest, a magical crystal known as the Forest Heart, had been taken by someone who had misunderstood its power. Without the crystal, the forest and the Watcher were slowly succumbing to the encroaching darkness.

Determined to save Everpine Forest, the children embarked on a quest to find the Forest Heart. Guided by the Watcher's wisdom, they navigated through hidden paths, solved ancient riddles, and overcame fearsome obstacles.

Their journey led them to a forgotten cave deep within the forest, where they found the Forest Heart, glowing with an otherworldly light. But guarding it was the darkness itself, a shadowy creature that thrived on fear and despair.

In a brave confrontation, they realized that the shadow creature was once a person, lost and scared, who had taken the Forest Heart in a misguided attempt to find their way out of the forest. Understanding and empathy broke the cycle of fear, and the shadowy figure transformed back into a lost traveler, grateful for their help.

The children returned the Forest Heart to the

Green-Eyed Watcher, restoring the forest's vitality and balance. The Watcher thanked them and disappeared into the depths of Everpine, its green eyes a comforting glow in the night.

Triumphant and filled with new respect for the natural world, the friends returned to their campsite, their hearts full of the night's extraordinary events. They shared their adventure around the campfire, turning the tale of The Eyes of the Forest into a legendary story in Pinebrook.

Their story became a symbol of bravery, compassion, and the enduring magic that lies in the heart of nature. Around the campfires, as the night whispered through the trees, their tale was told and retold, a thrilling and awe-inspiring reminder of the adventures that wait in the shadows and the power of unity in the face of the unknown.

"THE MYSTERY OF ECHOING HOLLOW"

In the small, picturesque town of Maplewood, nestled on the edge of the dense and foggy Whispering Woods, there was a legend that both intrigued and frightened the local children. The legend was about Echoing Hollow, a mysterious part of the woods where strange, unexplainable things happened, especially on nights when the fog was thickest.

The story, a favorite among campers at Camp Maplewood, told of ghostly echoes and shadows that moved with a life of their own in Echoing Hollow. It was said that these were the remnants of a forgotten village that once stood there, now hidden by the mists of time.

Twelve-year-old Sophie, her adventurous younger brother, Max, and their clever friend, Olivia, were captivated by this legend. One foggy evening, filled with a mix of excitement and trepidation, they decided to explore Echoing Hollow to uncover its secrets.

Armed with lanterns, a map, and walkie-talkies,

they ventured into the Whispering Woods. As they walked, the fog enveloped them, and the forest's usual sounds were muted, replaced by an eerie stillness. The deeper they went, the thicker the fog became, until they reached the edge of Echoing Hollow.

As they stepped into the Hollow, they heard faint whispers echoing through the trees, though no one was in sight. The whispers seemed to be calling out to them, leading them deeper into the mist.

Following the whispers, they came across the ruins of old stone houses, covered in moss and vines. It was the lost village, hidden for centuries. In the heart of the village was an ancient well, from which the whispers seemed to emanate.

As they approached the well, a cold wind swept through the Hollow, and ghostly figures appeared around them. The figures were the villagers, trapped in a spectral form, reliving their last moments over and over. The children realized these spirits were bound to the Hollow, unable to move on.

In the center of the village square, they found a

decrepit old book, its pages filled with the history of the village. The book revealed that the village had been cursed by a vengeful spirit, angry at the villagers for disturbing its resting place.

The only way to break the curse and free the spirits was to find a hidden amulet, the Heart of the Hollow, and return it to the spirit's tomb. Driven by a desire to help, Sophie, Max, and Olivia embarked on a quest to find the amulet.

Their search led them through forgotten pathways, under arches of intertwining branches, and into an abandoned chapel at the edge of the village. There, hidden beneath a floorboard, they found the amulet, glowing with a soft, eerie light.

As they retrieved the amulet, the spectral villagers gathered around them, their eyes filled with hope. The children returned to the well and, with a mix of fear and determination, placed the amulet inside.

A blinding light erupted from the well, illuminating the Hollow. The ghostly figures began to fade, their whispers turning into sighs of relief. As the last of the spirits disappeared, a peaceful calm settled over Echoing Hollow.

Exhausted but fulfilled, the children made their way back to camp, the fog lifting to reveal a starlit sky. They shared their incredible adventure by the campfire, turning the legend of Echoing Hollow into a tale of bravery, mystery, and the power of compassion.

Their story of The Mystery of Echoing Hollow became a legendary tale at Camp Maplewood, inspiring awe and wonder. Around the campfires, as the night wind whispered through the trees, their tale was told and retold, a thrilling and chilling reminder of the adventures that await in the shadows and the enduring bond of friendship in the face of the unknown.

"THE WHISPERING WILLOWS OF WICKERWOOD"

In the quaint, seemingly serene town of Elmwood, bordered by the ancient Wickerwood Forest, a spine-chilling legend was whispered among the children. This legend, often shared in hushed tones around campfires, was about the mysterious Whispering Willows of Wickerwood.

The story told of ghostly willow trees in a secluded part of the forest, known to murmur secrets of the past and future to those who dared to listen. It was said that these willows were the guardians of an ancient secret, and every fifty years, on a night when the stars aligned just right, they would reveal a hidden path to a forgotten part of the woods.

Curious and daring, 12-year-old Lucas, his fearless sister Lily, and their intelligent friend Emma, captivated by the legend, decided to brave Wickerwood on the fiftieth year. As the night of their adventure approached, the air in Elmwood grew thick with anticipation and whispered warnings from the elders.

Equipped with lanterns, a compass, and a hand-drawn map of the forest, they ventured into Wickerwood under the starlit sky. The deeper they went into the woods, the more the atmosphere changed. The air grew colder, and a dense fog began to blanket the ground, muffling their footsteps.

As they reached the heart of the forest, they found the Whispering Willows, their long branches swaying gently, even though there was no wind. The children felt an inexplicable chill run down their spines as they listened to the soft murmurs of the trees.

Following the whispers, they were led to a hidden grove, where an old, twisted tree stood, its bark covered in strange symbols. The murmurs grew louder, and the ground beneath the tree began to shimmer with a faint, eerie light.

Driven by an irresistible urge, Lucas, Lily, and Emma started to dig beneath the tree. Their hands unearthed an ancient wooden chest, bound by iron and adorned with more mysterious symbols. As they opened the chest, a gust of cold air escaped, and inside, they found a collection of old artifacts and a brittle parchment.

The parchment contained a prophecy about a great danger that would befall Elmwood, one that could only be averted by three brave souls who would find the chest. The children realized with a mix of fear and excitement that the prophecy was about them.

As they read on, the forest around them began to change. The fog lifted, revealing a hidden part of the woods, where shadows moved with a life of their own. The prophecy spoke of a shadow creature, born from the darkest part of the forest, that would seek to escape its confines on this very night.

Understanding their role in the legend, the children used the artifacts from the chest – each a talisman of light – to confront the shadow creature. As they held the talismans high, beams of light pierced the darkness, and the creature let out a piercing shriek, retreating back into the depths of the forest.

The children, though scared, felt a sense of triumph. They had averted the danger foretold in the prophecy. As they made their way back to the edge of the forest, the first light of dawn was breaking. The Whispering Willows stood silent now, their task complete.

Returning to Elmwood, Lucas, Lily, and Emma shared their incredible story. The tale of The Whispering Willows of Wickerwood became a legendary story in Elmwood, a tale of courage, mystery, and the unexpected role of fate.

Around campfires, as the night air rustled through the trees, their story was told and retold, a thrilling and haunting reminder of the adventures that lie hidden in the shadows, waiting for the brave and the bold to uncover them.

"THE LEGEND OF LANTERN LAKE"

In the small, picturesque town of Pine Hollow, surrounded by dense, evergreen forests and nestled at the foot of misty mountains, there lay a deep, dark lake known as Lantern Lake. The lake, shrouded in mystery and surrounded by ancient, towering pines, was the centerpiece of an eerie legend that sent shivers down the spines of the local children.

The story, a favorite among the kids at Pine Hollow Summer Camp, was about the mysterious Lantern Keeper of Lantern Lake. It was said that on nights when the fog rolled in thick over the lake, a ghostly figure holding a lantern could be seen wandering the shores, its light flickering through the mist.

Twelve-year-old Emily, her brave younger brother Sam, and their adventurous friend Alex were enthralled by this legend. As a thick fog began to envelop the town one cool autumn evening, they decided to venture to Lantern Lake to uncover the truth behind the mysterious Lantern Keeper.

Equipped with flashlights, a map, and a walkie-talkie, they set out towards the lake. As they approached, the fog grew thicker, swallowing the light from their flashlights, making the forest around them seem like a shadowy labyrinth.

Upon reaching the lake, they saw it - a faint light moving slowly along the lake's edge. Heart pounding with a mix of fear and curiosity, they followed the light from a safe distance. The eerie glow of the lantern cut through the fog, leading them around the lake to an old, forgotten cabin hidden among the trees.

As they neared the cabin, the lantern's light suddenly vanished, and the door to the cabin creaked open. Compelled by an irresistible urge to discover the cabin's secrets, they cautiously stepped inside.

The cabin was filled with old maps, strange artifacts, and a large, dusty book on a table. The book told the tale of the Lantern Keeper, once a lighthouse keeper who had vowed to guard the lake after his family had tragically drowned there. He had turned the lighthouse into a cabin, where he spent his days and nights watching over the lake, his lantern a beacon of his enduring vigil.

But the story took a dark turn. One stormy night, overcome by grief and loneliness, the Lantern Keeper ventured into the lake, intending to join his family in the depths. However, his spirit remained bound to the lake, cursed to wander its shores for eternity.

The children realized that the Lantern Keeper's spirit was trapped in sorrow, unable to find peace. The book spoke of a way to release his spirit - a locket belonging to the Keeper's family, lost in the depths of the lake.

Determined to help, Emily, Sam, and Alex embarked on a quest to find the locket. Guided by the old maps in the cabin, they used a rowboat to reach the deepest part of the lake. There, in the cold, dark waters, they found the locket, still glowing with a faint light.

As they brought the locket to the shore, the Lantern Keeper's ghostly figure appeared, his face twisted in anguish. Emily, mustering all her courage, approached and held out the locket. The Keeper's expression softened, and he reached out to take the locket.

As his fingers touched the locket, a blinding light enveloped the area. When the light faded, the children found themselves standing in broad daylight, the fog completely gone. The Lantern Keeper was nowhere to be seen.

Triumphant and relieved, they returned to the campsite, the sun shining brightly over Lantern Lake. They shared their incredible adventure, turning the tale of The Lantern Keeper into a legendary story of bravery, compassion, and the power of closure.

Their story, now a part of Pine Hollow's lore, was a reminder that sometimes the things we fear hide stories waiting to be heard. Around campfires, as the night wind whispered through the trees, their tale was told and retold, a gripping story of adventure, mystery, and the unexpected power of empathy in the face of the unknown.

"THE ECHOES OF MISTY HOLLOW"

In the quaint town of Cedar Grove, surrounded by dense, mist-covered hills, there was a place shrouded in mystery and fear - Misty Hollow. This hollow, a deep and shadowy valley, was the subject of an eerie legend that had been passed down through generations.

The story, a staple among the children of Cedar Grove, was about the haunting Echoes of Misty Hollow. It was said that on certain foggy nights, ghostly echoes could be heard throughout the valley, carrying with them whispers of an old, forgotten tale.

Twelve-year-old Mia, her courageous brother Jake, and their witty friend Liam were intrigued by this legend. On a particularly foggy autumn night, with a mix of excitement and apprehension, they decided to venture into Misty Hollow to discover the truth behind the ghostly echoes.

Armed with flashlights, a map, and walkie-talkies, they set out into the heart of the mist-covered valley. As they journeyed deeper, the fog grew thicker, muffling the sounds of the forest and casting eerie shadows among the trees.

As night fell, they reached a clearing where an old, abandoned mansion stood, its once grand structure now lost to time and nature. The mansion, known as Ravenwood Manor, was at the center of the legend.

The children, driven by a sense of adventure, entered the mansion. Inside, they found a grand hall filled with old portraits and dusty furniture. In the center of the hall was a large, ornate mirror, its surface clouded over the years.

As they explored further, they heard a soft, haunting melody echoing through the mansion. The music led them to a hidden room, where an old piano sat, playing on its own. Beside the piano was a diary, its pages yellowed with age.

The diary belonged to the last inhabitant of Ravenwood Manor, a young girl named Eliza, who had vanished mysteriously many years ago. The diary revealed that Eliza had discovered a secret passage in the mansion leading to an underground chamber, where a cursed artifact, known as the Heart of the Hollow, was kept.

Eliza wrote of how she had tried to remove the artifact to break the curse but instead became trapped in a realm between the living and the dead. She believed that only someone pure of heart could break the curse and free her spirit.

Realizing that the echoes were the cries of Eliza's trapped spirit, Mia, Jake, and Liam embarked on a quest to find the secret passage and the cursed artifact. Guided by the diary, they discovered the passage behind the mirror in the grand hall.

The passage led them to an underground chamber, where the Heart of the Hollow, a glowing gemstone, was kept. As they approached the artifact, the air grew colder, and ghostly figures began to emerge from the shadows, their whispers echoing off the chamber walls.

In a moment of bravery, Mia stepped forward and took the artifact. The chamber began to shake, and the ghostly figures converged on them. But instead of attacking, they circled around Mia, and a blinding light filled the room. When the light faded, they found themselves back in the clearing outside the mansion. The fog had lifted, revealing a starry sky. In the distance, they could see the faint figure of Eliza, smiling at them before vanishing into the night.

Triumphant but bewildered, the children returned to their campsite. They shared their adventure, turning the tale of The Echoes of Misty Hollow into a legendary story in Cedar Grove.

Their story became a reminder that sometimes the scariest legends hide a tale of bravery and redemption. Around the campfires, as the night wind rustled through the trees, their story was told and retold, a gripping and haunting tale of adventure, mystery, and the unexpected twists that await in the heart of the mist.